THE SMILING PETS™
Recipe Book

101 Easy-Make Treats

5 minutes or Less Prep Time!

Connie Fewell Reisenbigler
★**Author & Pet Chef**★

ISBN 0-9744445-1-0

Special thanks to Melanie Major, Sami J. Davies and
Marylou Draper for their professional editorial assistance.
John Kremer for his invaluable book expertise and guidance.

Cover Design: Scott Buchanan of rabidrobot.com

**The author wishes to acknowledge the following
pet-parents for their contributions of pictures and
support:** Margie Kinnard, Linda Ramsey, Jim & Barb Bishop, Jennifer
Bishop, David, Shannon McCully & family, Gary Fewell, Amy Castel,
Tony Melvin, Pam Steele & family, Cynthia Crow, Angela Brackey, Sylvia
& Tiffany Reisenbigler, Summer & Ariana Kolesar, Kathy McClanahan,
Sherry & Brandon Bahadorani, Sue Platek, Sue Hayes, Bob & Debbie
Lindgren, Sue Triptow, Greg Wingate, Nadine Roewer, George & Carol
Heck, Sam Davidson Family, Grace Fujikawa, Sandy Cottee Family, Lars
and Lise Nelson Family, Bill Sandell, Glanz Family, Jason & Cari Bates,
Shelly Booze, Liz & T.A. Hollis, Tom & Jeri Crawford, Toni Lackey Family
and Kevin, Freda Stanford, Cooper Tieaskie, Val Heinz, Darlene K.
Foster, Chris and Pat Childers, Rita Garry, Stan Jarosz, Amanda Dye,
Amy Roberts-Woodstock Veterinary Clinic, John Trapp, and Ericksons
Kennel Staff.

---

*"You can give without loving, but
you cannot love without giving."*

Carmichael

The Smiling Pets Recipe Book is available at your local
book store, pet store, and gift shop. Discounts on bulk
quantities can be ordered directly through
website: www.thesmilingpets.com or
call: 1-866-PET-LOVR

Contents

This book is dedicated
To our first family dog and little soul who taught
our family what a "pet-child" is.
To "Jonathan" Livingston Seagull,
and to the many pet children who bring
a sparkle to our eyes just to speak their names...
those still here, and those in Heaven.

Acknowledgments

It took a passion, not only for my pets, but for creating treats to compile *The Smiling Pets Recipe Book*. The inspiring quotes, collection of funny pet pictures, assortment of dog, cat, horse, tame and wild bird treats took a "tribe" of friends and family contributions.

I thank many for the positive energy sent my way in support. I found such joy in just discussing this project as it related to the many loves of our lives, our pet-children.

To begin with I was blessed with a great husband named Ardie, who is the "wind beneath my wings" with continuous praise and ideas. I value his advice and always have. I couldn't have even begun this project without my children— Sami J., with her recipe creation help and her professional writing help. My son, Dane, and daughter Karla .. sons-in law Mark Davies and Mark Paz, and granddaughter Paris Belle, who I love unconditionally. Eric, Shelley, Arden Reisenbigler and the Dick Anderson family of Austin, Texas. Parents, Dr. William Fewell, who as a Tulsa, Oklahoma natural health doctor-Chiropractor always believed in the Native American tradition of taking care of our pets and respecting them. My Mom, Pat Fewell, who loves her family and pet-children, too. My friend Beth Wirth, nicknamed "Mom," was a consistent source of help and always reliable. Bessy Psara is more than a friend, a true angel. Ayn Robbins and Vicki Tapp who always reminded me that I could do it. Although logically a bumblebee should not fly, it doesn't know it. I thank you so very much for believing in me.

Special thanks to Ron Lyons, Chief of Police for the Crystal Lake Park District, and Chief and Kasey, the "working dogs" and patrol dogs representative of America. Their work together in educating the public, search and rescue, drug sniffing, and protecting us was well represented by how graciously Ron offered to help in showing us this side of "pet families" too. I salute you and "the boys."

Thanks to celebrity songwriter, Carol Connors and her boys (Abyssian cats, past and present including M the Wonder Cat, Music and *NLYRICS) for her recommendation and lyrics for use in my book, song titled, *Unconditional Love, Unconditionally*. A beautiful song about the love of our pets. She believed in this "underdog" and is a winner in my book! I hope you will find *The Smiling Pets Recipe Book* not only a "treat" for its recipes, but let the pictures and quotes fill your soul and put a smile in your day… just like our companions and little people with fur do for us.

Picture Gallery

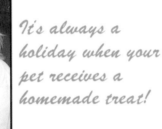

It's always a
holiday when your
pet receives a
homemade treat!

Christmas Joy
Be Yours!

The Andersons
Dick, Tami, Charlie, Olivia,
Lindsey and Johnny Texas

Introduction

◆◆◆

Over the past few years, I've noticed that the Christmas cards we've received include pictures of pets along with the family. Actually, some cards feature only pets. Sometimes an announcement of a new birth arrives in the mail, along with an announcement of a new pet addition to the family.

I hope one day to be the person my pets think I am...

The distinction between human children and pet-children has blurred. This is a good thing, I think. I have never seen a picture of a family, with their pets included, who didn't have a smile that went straight from the eyes to the soul. Even the names given pet-children have changed. Instead of Rover or Spot, we name our pets Winston, Charlie (my smiling dog), Cory, Lady Freckles, Bart, Teq, Bailey, Johnny Texas or Ambersue, reflecting our family love for our pet-children.

As our pets become our children, we learn that tasty, healthy, nutritious food is as important for our pet-family members as it is for our human family. Homemade treats allow pet-parents to make snacks that are healthy with no artificial preservatives. Store-bought treats are practical at times, but nothing compares to the aroma of fresh baked treats for pet-children. A three minute preparation of turkey, veal, or beef baby food cookies for your dog, cat , or a homemade treat for your horse or bird is an act of love for their companionship and loyalty.

Since time is a precious commodity in our family, my daughter, Sami J., and I created and tweaked all of *The Smiling Pets* recipes to make sure the preparation time is five minutes or less. They are simple enough that even a child can easily prepare them. The recipes are varied since dogs, cats, horses, and birds deserve a "tweet" now and then, too. Try the *Krunchy Kritter* doggie donuts, Crabmeat Crème Brulee for your cat, or Cherry Pie Suet Treats for birds, and Apple Snax for horses. All in our "neigh"borhood love these treats!

It's that simple. I suggest using these recipes as a guideline and template, but exchanging what you feel is healthy, available in your cupboard at home, and to your pet's individual taste. Soy and rice milk are healthy alternatives to replace milk on any recipe. Homemade pet treats are also great gift ideas for the pet-parent who adores their pet, or a gift for the pet-loving friend who has it all, except a treat recipe book to share with their beloved companion.

The inspirational quotes in *The Smiling Pets Recipe Book* are credited to the source, unless we were unable to determine the author. If I missed crediting someone please e-mail me and I will add your name to the quote.

The personal family pictures of my "tribe" of friends speak for themselves. Pets speak the language of unconditional love. Cooking for my pet-children satisfies my need to care for them, as I hope it does for you. "Bone" appetit!

The Smiling Pets Mom,
Connie Fewell Reisenbigler

Connie

Dog Treats

A Faithful Dog

A faithful dog will play with you
and laugh with you, or cry.
He'll gladly starve to stay with you
nor ever reason why.
And when you're feeling out of sorts
somehow he'll understand.
He'll watch you with his shining eyes
and try to lick yur hand.
His blind, implicit faith in you
is matched by his great love -
The kind that all of us should have
in the Master up above.
When everything is said and done
I guess this isn't odd
For when you spell "dog" backwards
you get the name of God.

Author Unknown

Apple of My Eye Pupcakes

Prep Time: 4 minutes   Bake Time: 15 - 18 minutes

Sweet treats and healthy, too!

1/2 cup of unsweetened applesauce
1 cup of water
1/2 teaspoon vanilla
2 eggs beaten
2 cups of whole wheat flour
1/2 cup of honey or molasses
1 tablespoon of baking powder
Dab on cream cheese

MIX all ingredients thoroughly, and make sure dry mixture blends well.

POUR into greased muffin pan and place into a 350° F preheated oven.

BAKE for 15 - 18 minutes. Insert toothpick to check if done. Dab on cream cheese and serve. Makes 1 dozen large, or 2 dozen small pupcakes.

"Dog lovers are a good breed themsleves."
    Gladys Taber

Baby Food Soft Dog Cookies

Prep Time: 3 minutes   Bake Time: 12 - 15 minutes

This simple cookie recipe can be made using turkey, beef, chicken, or veal... whatever your four-legged pet desires. Great for the older dog, easy on their teeth.

3 jars of Stage 2 (2-1/2 oz size) meat baby food
1 cup of nonfat dry milk (powdered milk)
1 cup of wheat germ
1 egg
2 tablespoons of flour

PREHEAT oven to 375ºF . Mix above ingredients, blending well.
DROP by tablespoon on lightly greased cookie sheet.
BAKE for 12 - 15 minutes or until brown and let cool. Store in refrigerator.

As Oprah once said about her pet-children, Sophie and Solomon-- "What dogs? These are my childen, little people with fur who make our hearts open a little wider." I agree!

Bacon Bonanza Bones

Prep Time: 4 minutes   Bake Time: 35 - 40 minutes

1/2 cup of milk
3 cups of whole wheat flour
1/2 cup of water
1 egg
4 tablespoons of melted bacon fat
1 tablespoon of bacon, cut up pieces
1/4 teaspoon of onion or garlic powder

MIX all ingredients thoroughly, until free of lumps. Add additional flour to make the mixture stiff, if needed.
PINCH off 2-inch pieces of dough and roll into balls OR cut out with dog bone cutter or any other cookie cutter design. Place onto a well-greased cookie sheet.
BAKE at 350°F for 35 - 40 minutes. Let cool, then serve.

The Airedale, an unrivaled mixture of brains and clownish wit.
Ingredients one looks for in a spouse!
Chip Brown, Connoisseur *Magazine*

Banana Muttcakes

Prep Time: 4 minutes   Bake Time: 20 minutes

A change of pace... a desirable taste!

2 bananas--mashed
3 tablespoons of honey
1 egg
1 teaspoon of vanilla
2-1/2 cups of flour
1 teaspoon of baking powder
1-1/2 cups of water

MIX all ingredients thoroughly.
POUR into greased muffin pans and place into a 350° F preheated oven.
BAKE for 20 minutes, or until brown. Cool and serve. Best to refrigerate or freeze to serve later. Makes 1 dozen large muttcakes, or 3 dozen mini-cakes.

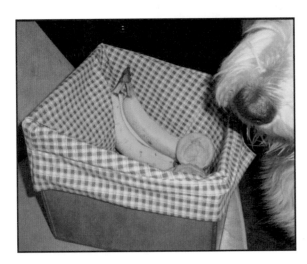

Caught in the act!

Bitsy Bacon Bites

Prep Time: 5 minutes   Bake Time: 28 ~ 30 minutes

Pleasin' to smell, and tasty to eat...

1/3 cup of bacon drippings or vegetable oil
2 cups of flour
1/2 cup of milk
1 egg
3~4 slices of bacon, crushed
1 teaspoon of garlic powder
1/2 cup of cold water
1/3 cup of softened cream cheese

MIX all ingredients thoroughly, except the cream cheese.

DROP into teaspoon~sized biscuits on a lightly greased pan and place into a 350° F preheated oven.

BAKE for 28 ~ 30 minutes. Dab cream cheese on top of biscuit after it has cooled, then serve. Makes 1 dozen large biscuits.

"Dogs are not our whole life, but they make our lives whole."
Unknown

Canned Dog Food Delight Biscuits

Prep Time: 4 minutes   Bake Time: 18 - 20 minutes

Turn your pet's favorite canned dog food into simple-to-make biscuit treats!

1 15-ounce can of your pet's favorite nutritious canned dog food
1/2 cup of wheat germ
1/2 cup of nonfat dry milk
1 egg

Note: As an option sprinkle grated cheddar cheese and/or bovine colostrum (found in health food stores) over warm cookies.

MIX all ingredients thoroughly.

BAKE at 375°F for 18 - 20 minutes. Let cool, then serve.

My pet-child
Charlie...smiling

"I know that dogs are pack animals, but it is difficult to imagine a pack of standard poodles.. and if there was such a thing as a pack of standard poodles, where would they rove to? Bloomingdales?"

Yvonne Clifford

Healthy Carrot Cheezy Muffins

Prep Time: 4 minutes   Bake Time: 20 - 25 minutes

Yummy to doggy's tummy!

2 eggs
1 cup of milk
3 cups of all-purpose flour
2 tablespoons of baking powder
1 cup of cheddar cheese-shredded
1 cup of carrots-finely grated

MIX all ingredients thoroughly.

POUR into greased muffin tins 3/4 full, and place into a 350° F preheated oven.

BAKE for 20 - 25 minutes, or until golden brown. Cool and serve. Makes about 1 dozen large muffins, or 2 dozen small muffins.

A Perfect Day!

Celebration Cake!

Prep Time: 4 minutes   Bake Time: 25 - 28 minutes

Perfect treat for a job well done!

1-1/2 cups of flour
1 13-ounce can of dog food
(any flavor, your choice)
1/2 cup of beef liver, chopped
into small bite pieces
2 eggs
1/2 cup of softened cream
cheese
Note: A tasty icing for your pet-child's
cake is to mix meat baby food with
cream cheese.

SAUTE or microwave liver in

butter or margarine until fully cooked, then chop.

MIX all ingredients thoroughly, except the cream
cheese.

POUR into a greased 9-inch round cake pan, and
place into a 325° F preheated oven.

BAKE for 25 - 28 minutes until golden brown. Cool,
then frost with cream cheese. Makes 1 large cake (to
share).

Did someone say treat?

Cheesy Peanut Butter Drop Cookies

Prep Time: 5 minutes   Bake Time: 10 - 12 minutes

Tail waggin' good... can't eat just one!

2 cups of flour
1 cup of milk
1/2 cup of creamy or chunky peanut butter
1/4 cup of grated Parmesan cheese
2 teaspoons baking powder
1 egg
2 teaspoons chicken broth

MIX flour and milk until it's a doughy consistency. Add the rest of the ingredients, folding in egg.
DROP into teaspoon-sized portions on a cookie sheet and place into a 350° F preheated oven.
BAKE for 10 - 12 minutes or until golden brown. Cool, then serve. Makes 1 dozen cookies.

"Even the tiniest poodle is lionhearted, ready to defend home, master, and mistress."
Louis Sabin

Cheesy Pups Dog Bones

Prep Time: 5 minutes   Bake Time: 10 ~ 15 minutes

Great bone treat for pups or adult pet-children

2 cloves of garlic, minced well
1/2 cup of vegetable oil
1/2 cup of shredded cheddar cheese
2-1/2 cups of regular or whole wheat flour
1/2 cup of water
1/8 cup of dried parsley
1 egg

MIX all ingredients (except water) until it is the consistency of coarse meal, then SLOWLY add the water until the mixture is doughy and can be formed into balls. OR, flatten out the dough, adding more flour a little bit at a time to make the dough stiff and 1/2 inch thickness. Spread out on a floured surface.

CUT OUT shapes of dog bones or characters and place into a 375° F preheated oven.

BAKE for 10 ~ 15 minutes or until light brown. Cool, then serve or store in the refrigerator. Makes 1 dozen bones.

"My little dog--a heartbeat at my feet."
      Edith Wharton

Chocolate Less Lab-Chip Bones

Prep Time: 4 minutes   Bake Time: 20 - 25 minutes

Very easy, and a creative way to share with beloved pet-children.
One of the most favorite treats for pet-parents--
Chocolate Lab-Chip cookies!
Note: NO Chocolate Please! It can be toxic or upsetting to their tummies.

1/2 cup of cut up pieces of turkey jerky or beef jerky
2/3 cup of melted butter
1 egg beaten
2 cups of whole
wheat flour
1-1/4 cups of water
1/2 cup of cornmeal

MIX melted butter, egg, flour, water and cornmeal.

FOLD IN the turkey or beef jerky pieces, adding flour as needed to make the dough stiff. Flatten dough to 1/2 inch thick, and using bone or character cutters, create shapes to place on a greased cookie sheet. Place in pre-heated 375° F oven.

BAKE for 20 - 25 minutes. Cool, then serve. Store in the refrigerator and serve leftovers another day, or share with a buddy next door! Makes 2 dozen bones.

"A dog teaches a boy fidelity, perseverance, and to turn around three times before lying down."
                    Robert Benchley

Connie's "Freedom" Toast Doggie Bites

Prep Time: 3 minutes   Cooking Time: 4 minutes

Breakfast, lunch, or dinnertime snack.

1 egg
1 slice of bread (whole wheat or white)
3 teaspoons of bacon drippings
1/4 cup of grated cheese

MIX egg, cheese, and bacon drippings in a small bowl.
PLACE bread in bowl, flipping sides until egg mixture
has saturated bread.
COOK bread on greased pan over the stove, flipping
over until sides are brown.
COOL then cut in small pieces and serve! Makes 1
serving.

*"You can say any foolish thing to a dog, and the dog will give you a look
that says, 'My God, you're RIGHT! I NEVER would have thought of that!"*
Dave Barry

Crunchy Baked Yam Chips

Prep Time: 5 minutes   Bake Time: 15 - 18 minutes

Not just a southern treat cookie... yummy yammy!

2 medium-sized fresh yams
4 tablespoons of honey
1 egg
1/2 cup of cream of wheat
1/2 cup of nonfat dry milk (powdered milk)

MICROWAVE yams until soft (about 3 minutes), then mash with a potato masher.

MIX all ingredients until blended, then drop by spoonful onto greased cookie sheet. Place in preheated oven at 350°F.

BAKE for 15 - 18 minutes, or until brown. Cool and serve. Makes 2 dozen yam chips.

"If your pet-child is a bit chunky then you're not getting enough exercise!"

Fleas Be Gone Dog Bones

Prep Time: 5 minutes   Bake Time: 20 - 25 minutes

Helps rid dogs of fleas with treats sure to please!

2 cups of flour
1 cup of corn meal
1/2 cup of wheat flour
2 tablespoons of garlic powder or
2 cloves minced garlic
1/2 teaspoon of salt
3 tablespoons of olive oil
2 eggs
1 cup chicken, beef, or vegetable
stock bouillion

MIX all ingredients, adding more flour, a little bit at a time if needed, to make a firm consistency. Spread dough out on floured surface.

SHAPE "bones" with cookie cutters and place onto a greased cookie sheet in a preheated 400°F oven.

BAKE 20-25 minutes.

"A watchdog is a dog kept to guard your home, usually by sleeping where a burglar would awaken the household by falling over him."

Unknown

Frozen Peanut Butter Yogurt Blitz

Prep Time: 2 minutes

Your pet-children willl love this treat after a long hot day in the sun, or a stroll in the park.

1 6-ounce container of vanilla yogurt
1/2 cup peanut butter
1/2 cup of milk or soymilk

MELT peanut butter in the microwave for 1 minute on high.
MIX all ingredients.
POUR into ice cube tray and freeze. Serve yogurt cubes in a bowl on a hot summer day or for an afternoon protein treat!

"Even the tiniest poodle or chihuahua is still a wolf at heart."

Dorothy Hinshaw Patent,
Dogs: The Wolf Within

Fruity Yogurt Treats

Prep Time: 1 minute

Refreshingly cool, icy treat!

1 8-ounce container of strawberry yogurt
1 (2-1/2-ounce) jar of fruit baby food
2 mashed kiwis or strawberries

MIX ingredients together.
POUR mixture into ice cube tray.
FREEZE overnight, then serve. A nice treat for your pet-children.

"In order to keep a true perspective of one's importance, everyone should have a dog that will worship him and a cat that will ignore him."

Dereke Bruce, Taipei, Taiwan

Garlic Chunk Cheezy Bones

Prep Time: 4 minutes   Bake Time: 12 minutes

Cheese please...

1-1/2 cups of Parmesan, cheddar, or Swiss grated cheese
1 cup of whole wheat flour
1 cup of softened butter or margarine
2 tablespoons of minced garlic
1/2 cup of milk
1 egg

CREAM together the cheese and margarine or butter.
ADD garlic and flour and mix thoroughly. Mix in milk, then add additional flour as needed to make dough stiff.
CUT OUT bone shapes, or other shapes, to please your pet-child. Place on greased cookie sheet in a pre-heated 375° F oven.
BAKE for 12 minutes. Makes 1 dozen bones.
Refrigerate.

"The dog was created especially for children. He is the God of frolic."
   Henry Ward Beecher

Healthy Pet Shake

Prep Time: 3 minutes   Blend Time: 1 minute

Working dog or lap dog...

1 cup of milk (regular or soy)
1/4 cup of honey
1/2 banana
1/2 cup of plain yogurt
1 cube of chicken or beef bouillon
1 egg

BLEND all ingredients together, then serve!

Note: As an option add 1/4 cup of bovine colostrum powder (found in health food stores). An excellent source of protein, energy, and immune boost for our pets!

*A milk moustache. What I
will do for my pet-mom...*
                        Winston

Iced Doggie Popsicles

Prep Time: 2 minutes

Cool treat for a hot summer day!

5 small chopped pieces of chicken or beef
2 cubes of chicken or beef bouillon
1 cup of water

DISSOLVE bouillon in water and combine with meat pieces.

POUR mixture into an ice tray.

FREEZE overnight, then serve! Makes 1 serving.

"Children and dogs are as necessary to the welfare of the country as Wall Street and the railroads."

Harry S. Truman

Meatball Treatball

Prep Time: 4 minutes   Saute Time: 6 minutes

Tasty, healthy bits of protein

1/2 pound of ground beef, ground chuck, or ground turkey
2 tablespoons of garlic powder
1/2 cup of cooked rice
1/4 cup of grated carrots

MIX all ingredients, then form into balls.
SAUTE the meatballs until brown and thoroughly cooked.
COOL then serve. Refrigerate leftovers to serve another day, or with your pet-child's daily meal. Makes 2 servings.

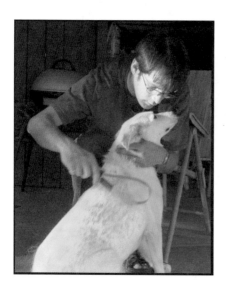

"...none are as fiercely loyal as dog people. In return, no doubt, for the never-ending loyalty of dogs."

Linda Shrieves,
Orlando Sentinel

Krunchy Kritter™
Doggie Donuts

Prep Time: 5 minutes   Bake Time: 18 ~ 20 minutes

Pet-children love donuts, too!

2 cups of flour
2 eggs
3 tablespoons of honey
3 tablespoons of peanut butter
(crunchy preferred, but creamy
is okay)
1/3 cup of vegetable shortening
3 teaspoons of baking soda
Dash of salt
3/4 cup of oats
1~1/2 teaspoons of vanilla

Note: As an option, sprinkle bovine colostrum powder (found in health food stores) on donuts for a healthy boost and extra protein! Makes 1 dozen donuts and donut holes.

MICROWAVE honey and peanut butter together until runny (20 seconds).

MIX all ingredients together, including the honey and peanut butter mixture. Shape into 12 balls, then flatten. Use a bottle cap to make the donut holes, or cookie cutter to shape treats. Place shapes onto a greased cookie sheet in a preheated 350° F oven.

BAKE for 18 ~ 20 minutes.

Daddy's girl!

Liver Bites

Prep Time: 3 minutes   Bake Time: 15 - 18 minutes

Bits and bites of total doggie delight!

1/2 cup of cooked chicken livers
1-3/4 cup of cornmeal
2 eggs
3 tablespoons of molasses or honey
2 tablespoons of minced garlic

BLEND all ingredients in blender or food processor.
POUR mixture into a greased medium-sized baking
pan. Place in a preheated 400° F oven.
BAKE for 15 - 18 minutes, or until toothpick comes out
clean. Cool, then serve. Refrigerate leftovers to serve later.

"Things that upset a Terrier may pass
virtually unnoticed by a Great Dane."
Smiley Blanton

Meaty Crunchy Dog Bones

Prep Time: 5 minutes   Bake Time: 25 - 30 minutes

Great to spice up any meaty meal!

1/4 cup of chicken or beef broth
1 (2-1/2 ounce) jar of any meat baby food
1/2 cup of water
1 tablespoon of honey
1 tablespoon of parsley
1-1/2 cups of flour
1 egg beaten
1/2 cup of nonfat dry milk
1/4 cup of oatmeal

MIX all ingredients together.

ROLL dough onto floured surface, and cut into bone or animal shapes. Arrange shapes on greased cookie sheet and place into a preheated 350° F oven.

BAKE for 25 - 30 minutes. Let cool. Freeze or refrigerate to last for many days of treat time! Makes 1 dozen bones.

"If you think dogs can't count, try putting three dog biscuits in your pocket, then giving Fido only two of them."

Phil Pastoret

Mighty Dog Cheese Balls

Prep Time: 4 minutes   Bake Time: 20 - 25 minutes

This snack treat can be adjusted to fit the desires of your pet-child.

2 cups of Betty Crocker^R Bisquick Mix
1/2 cup of grated cheese (cheddar or swiss)
1/2 cup of finely chopped cooked meat (bacon, steak, chicken, or lamb)
3/4 cup of milk
2 tablespoons of bacon grease

MIX all ingredients together in a bowl until doughy.
DROP mixture by spoonfuls onto a greased cookie sheet, and place in a preheated 350° F oven.
BAKE for 20 - 25 minutes, or until golden brown. Cool, then serve. Makes 2 dozen Mighty Dog Cheese Balls.

*This dog deserves a bone...
a real one.*

Mint Coconut Doggie Breath Biscuits

Prep Time: 5 minutes   Bake Time: 15 minutes

Mint and coconut--freshens the breath and flosses the teeth naturally!

4 tablespoons of vegetable oil
1 egg beaten
2 tablespoons of chopped mint or parsley leaves
2 teaspoons of mint extract
2 cups of flour
3/4 cup of milk (regular, soy, or rice milk)
1/4 cup of shredded coconut

MIX all ingredients together.

DROP heaping tablespoons of dough onto a greased cookie sheet. Place in a preheated 375° F oven.

BAKE for 15 minutes, or until golden brown. Cool, then serve.

Sami J. and adopted pet-child, Ciwyn, from the Reno, Nevada ASPCA

"If you can't decide between a Shepherd, a Setter, or a Poodle, just get them all. Adopt a mutt!"

ASPCA

Mutt Party Mix

Prep Time: 2 minutes

Make any party special with treats for your pet-children!

2-1/2 cups of Chex Mix
2-1/2 cups of Cheerios
1/2 cup of cheese powder
1/2 cup of melted butter or margarine
1 package of dry brown gravy mix
1 cup of beef jerky, chopped into small pieces

POUR melted butter or margarine into a 13"x9" pan.
STIR in ingredients. Cool, then serve.

"Dogs have given their absolute all. We are the center of their universe; we are the focus of their love and faith and trust. They serve us in return for scraps. It is without a doubt the best deal man has ever made."

Roger Caras

No Bake Crispy Treats

Prep Time: 5 minutes

This is by far one of the easiest to make because there is nothing to bake!

1 cup of miniature marshmallows, melted or marshmallow creme
1/4 cup of margarine OR butter
1/2 cup of peanut butter
2 cups of Rice Krispies cereal
1/4 cup of bacon bits
Note: mixture can also be pressed into a greased 13" x 9" pan. Makes about 1/2 dozen treats.

MELT together marshmallows, margarine, and peanut butter in saucepan over low heat stirring occasionally until smooth. Or microwave until melted--about 2 minutes.

POUR mixture over combined cereal and bacon bits (save some for the smiley face), tossing lightly until thoroughly coated. With greased fingers, gently shape into 1-1/2" balls.

FINISH by placing balls onto waxed paper. Cool at room temperature until set, then serve. Refrigerate leftovers to serve another day.

No Bake Hors D'ogs

Prep Time: 3 minutes

Doggone Doglicious!

1/2 cup grated cheese
3 tablespoons of vegetable shortening
1 finely sliced beef hot dog
1/2 cup oatmeal

MIX together all ingredients, except oatmeal.

FORM mixture into a log shape. Roll log over oatmeal, then refrigerate.

SLICE into half-inch rounds, then serve. Yummy.

"There is no psychiatrist in the world like a puppy licking your face."

Bern Williams

Oatmeal Doggie Cookies

Prep Time: 5 minutes   Bake Time: 15-20 minutes

Oatmeal--not just for breakfast anymore

1-1/4 cups flour
2 tablespoons of vegetable oil
or melted butter
1/4 cup of honey or molasses
1/4 cup of shredded fine
carrots
1 cup of water
1/2 tablespoon of unsweetened applesauce
1/2 cup of cooked rice
1/2 cup of instant oatmeal

MIX all ingredients thoroughly.
DROP on greased cookie sheet by the spoonful, or
cookie cutter shapes. Place in preheated 375° F oven.
BAKE 15 - 20 minutes or until brown. Cool, then
serve. Makes 2 dozen small cookies, or 1 dozen cutout
shapes.

*"A dog is the only thing on
earth that loves you more
than you love yourself."*
Josh Billings

Oh Muttz Oh Balls

Prep Time: 4 minutes   Cooking Time: 3 minutes

Holiday or any day treat

1-1/2 cups of crushed premium dry dog food
1 teaspoon of cooking oil
2 eggs
2/3 cup of cold water
1 cup of cream of chicken soup
1 teaspoon of garlic powder

MIX all ingredients (except soup and cold water) in a blender.

FORM into 1/2-inch balls. Bring water to a rolling boil in a 1 quart pan, and add soup.

DROP balls into boiling soup/water. Let stew for 3 minutes. Remove, drain some of the soup, then cool. Refrigerate and serve.

Say Cheese!

Pigs in a Blanket

Prep Time: 2 minutes   Bake Time: 15-18 minutes

Fun to make treat for your pet-children to eat!

3 slices of ham
1 cylinder of Pillsbury biscuits
Optional: cream cheese or grated cheese

POP open the biscuits. Flatten each biscuit out on an ungreased cookie sheet. Cut ham into pieces to fit inside biscuit when rolled.
PLACE ham pieces inside each biscuit, then roll each up into a hotdog shape. Place in preheated 375° F oven.
BAKE 15 - 18 minutes or until brown. Cool. Spread cream cheese or grated cheese over biscuits, then serve.

Quick Quiche for Dogs

Prep Time: 5 minutes   Bake Time: 28 - 32 minutes

Good treat to serve when more than 1 pet-child is at home, or some pet-cousins are over to visit. Not your ordinary treat, but neither are our pet-children. Pet-parents LOVE this, too!

2/3 cup of milk
4 eggs
1 frozen pie crust, ready-made
1/2 cup of cheddar or
Parmesan cheese
1 teaspoon of garlic powder
1/2 cup of broccoli

Note: This is a good treat to be creative with and add or substitute what your pet-child loves!

MIX all ingredients thoroughly, beating eggs and blending well.

POUR into frozen pie shell. Place into preheated 375° F oven.

BAKE 28 - 32 minutes or until golden brown. Use a toothpick to confirm doneness. Cool, then cut into pie pieces and serve. Refrigerate leftovers to share with a pet-friend, or serve again another day!

"There's only one smartest dog in the world, and every boy has it."

Unknown

Quick Zap Snack

Prep Time: 5 minutes   Microwave time: 4 minutes

Tasty... quick treat!

3 tablespoons of oatmeal
3/4 cup of beef or chicken broth
2-1/2 cups of whole wheat flour
1 egg slightly beaten
1 teaspoon of garlic powder
Optional: 1/2 cup of softened cream cheese to dab on top
of cooled snack

MIX together flour, egg, and broth in a bowl. Then
blend in oatmeal and garlic powder.

ROLL into ball shapes by hand, or flatten dough to use
cookie cutters to shape. Arrange the dough on a sheet of
parchment (or waxed) paper in a single layer to be placed
in the microwave.

ZAP (microwave) on high for 4 minutes or until firm.
Let cool until
hardened.

*"What counts is not necessarily
the size of the dog in the fight--
it's the size of the fight in the
dog."*

Dwight D. Eisenhower

Tater Treats for Dogs

Prep Time: 2 minutes

Great treat from leftover mashed potatoes!

1-1/2 cups of mashed potatoes
1/4 cup of finely grated carrots
1 egg
2 tablespoons of flour

MIX ingredients, patting on flour after mixture is well blended.

ROLL dough out to a 1/4-inch thickness. Cut with cookie cutters or shape into round balls; flatten into pancake shapes.

SAUTE and brown on each side. Cool, then serve. Makes 1 serving for a large dog, and 2 servings for a small dog.

"Dogs feel very strongly that they should always go with you in the car, in case the need should arise for them to bark violently at nothing right in your ear."
Dave Barry

Victory Veggie Vittles

Prep Time: 3 minutes   Bake Time: 10 - 12 minutes

Healthy and tasty, too. Great for vegetarian families!

1/2 cup of applesauce
1/2 cup of grated carrots or green beans
1 egg beaten
1/2 cup of cooked rice
1/2 cup of clear broth or water
3/4 cup of flour

MIX all ingredients well.

DROP by rounded teaspoons onto a greased cookie sheet. Place in a preheated 350° F oven.

BAKE 10 - 12 minutes. Cool, then serve. Best refrigerated after baking.

Who loves ya baby!

43

Treats for Tricks
Pumpkin Cookies

Prep Time: 3 minutes   Bake Time: 15 - 20 minutes

A welcome change from the everyday bone treat!

2 cups (or one 15-ounce can) of pure pumpkin puree
3/4 cup of cream of wheat cereal
2 teaspoons of honey
3/4 cup of powdered milk
1 egg

MIX all ingredients together.

DROP by spoonful of dough onto a greased cookie sheet. Place in preheated 350° F oven.

BAKE 15 - 20 minutes. Cool, then serve. Refrigerate or freeze to thaw and serve next treat time. Makes 2 dozen cookies.

"If you're a dog and your owner suggests that you wear a sweater... suggest that he wear a tail."

Fran Liebowitz

Turkey Drumstick Bone Dips

Prep Time: 5 minutes

Dippity do dog dips... kind of like a cold fondue treat for your pet-child

3 nutritious homemade or store-bought healthy dog (milk) bones
1/2 cup of honey or molasses
3/4 cup of Rice Krispies cereal
1/2 cup of creamy peanut butter
2 tablespoons of bacon bits

DIP one end of each dog bone in bowl with peanut butter.
SPREAD a light coating of
honey or molasses on same end of bone.
ROLL the same end on a bed of Rice Krispies with bacon bits, then serve to your waiting wagger! Refrigerate and serve leftovers later, OR make a single serve treat!

"The pug is living proof that God has a sense of humor."
Margot Kanthem,
American Writer

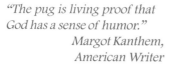

Vitality Vegi-Bits

Prep Time: 5 minutes   Bake Time: 30 minutes

Healthy vegetarian treat, and tasty, too!

3 cups of flour
1 cup of powdered milk
3/4 cup of vegetable oil
3 tablespoons of brown sugar
1 can of cream of mushroom soup
1 can (or 1 cup) of water
2 eggs
1/2 cup of diced carrots

MIX all ingredients, then shape into a ball and roll out
to 1/4-inch thickness.
CUT into any shape you prefer, such as a bone shape
or strips. Place shapes on an ungreased cookie sheet, then
put in a preheated 325° F oven.
BAKE for 30 minutes or until brown. Cool, then serve.
Best refrigerated. Makes 2 to 2-1/2 dozen Vegi-Bits.

*"There's just something about
dogs that makes you feel
good. You come home, they're
thrilled to see you. They are
good for the ego."*
                    Janet Schnellman

46

Cat Treats

"Dogs eat. Cats dine."
Ann Taylor

A Meal for the Mature

Prep Time: 2 minutes

A perfect delight for the more mature kitties in your life!

1/2 cup of leftover chicken or chicken pieces
4 teaspoons of grated cheese
1/2 cup of water
1 bouillon cube

POUR 1/2 cup of warm water over bouillon cube and stir to dissolve.

ADD shredded chicken to the mix to make a soupy combination.

SPRINKLE the grated cheese over the soup and serve.

"The smart cat doesn't let on that he is."
H. G. Frommer

Anchovy Wrap for Kitty Cats

Prep Time: 2 minutes

Jazzy loves this treat!

1 fresh or freeze-dried anchovy
1 slice bread
1/2 cup of cream, or soy milk (can be warmed)

WRAP the anchovy in the bread.
POUR on cream or milk, then serve. It's that easy, and your cat will lap it up!

Baby Food Kit Cat Treats

Prep Time: 4 minutes   Bake Time: 15 minutes

Purr-fect treat to make quick !

3 (2-1/2 ounce) jars of stage 2 turkey (or any meat) baby food
1/2 cup of wheat germ
1/2 cup of nonfat dry milk
1 egg beaten
1/4 cup of chopped fine carrots
Note: Carrots are a healthy, natural tartar remover for pet-children kittens and cats.

MIX all ingredients together.

FORM into 12 small balls, then flatten each ball on a greased cookie sheet. Place in preheated 350° F oven.

BAKE for 15 minutes or until brown. Cool, then serve. Refrigerate leftovers!

"The smallest feline is a masterpiece."
Leonardo DaVinci

Bessy's Christmas Treat Balls

Prep Time: 4 minutes

As much fun to make as it is for Miss Kitty to receive!

1 cup of mashed cooked pumpkin, or canned unspiced pumpkin puree
2 teaspoons of cod liver oil
2 teaspoons of kelp
1 teaspoon of catnip
1 cup of minced turkey or shredded chicken
1 toasted piece of sliced bread, or 1 cup of salad croutons crumbled into pieces.

MIX together, blending all ingredients well.

ROLL into balls and chill.

FEED as treats at Christmas, or any time of the year.

Best refrigerated. Makes about 1 dozen treats.

"Cats are connoisseurs of comfort."
James Herriot

Cat Cookies

Prep Time: 4 minutes   Bake Time: 18 - 20 minutes

A satisfying treat goes great with a cold bowl of milk!

1 (7-ounce) can of mashed sardines or flake tuna
1/2 cup of nonfat dry milk (powdered milk)
1/2 cup of wheat germ or cream of wheat cereal
1 egg
2 tablespoons of flour
6 freeze-dried sardines (can be cut in half) for topper
Note: Dab on cream cheese after cookies cool for easy placement
of sardines or tuna.

MIX ingredients in a bowl. Roll into 12 shapes. Flatten.

PLACE on lightly greased cookie sheet and put in

preheated 350° F oven.

BAKE 18 - 20 minutes or until brown. Refrigerate

leftovers. Makes about 1 dozen cookies.

Cat Egg Snax

Prep Time: 2 minutes   Microwave Time: 20 seconds

Good morning, sunny side up!

1/2 cup of milk
1/2 cup of grated Swiss cheese
1 egg
1/2 teaspoon of catnip

MIX well in microwave cooking bowl.
MICROWAVE on high for 20 seconds. Cool, then serve!

"Cats are absolute individuals, with their own ideas about everything, including the people they own."

John Dingman

Chicken and Biscuit Balls

Prep Time: 4 minutes   Bake Time: 18 minutes

The aroma of this treat fills the home with cheer!

3/4 cup of bisquick mix
3/4 cup of cornmeal
1 cup of shredded cooked
chicken (good use for
 leftover chicken)
2 tablespoons of softened, or
melted, butter or margarine
3/4 cup of chicken broth (or 2
cubes of bouillon and 1/2 cup
of warm water)

MIX all ingredients. Roll dough into about 20 balls.
PLACE on greased cookie sheet and put in preheated

350° F oven.

BAKE approximately 18 minutes. Cool, then serve. Can
share with the neighbor's cat or refrigerate what's left, if
there is any left! Makes about 2 dozen treats.

*"Authors like cats because they are such quiet,
lovable, wise creatures and cats like authors for the
same reasons."*

Robertson Davies

Cat Egg Salad

Prep Time: 4 minutes

Now you can enjoy breakfast with your pet-child!

1 pinch of garlic powder
2 tablespoons of powdered milk
2 drops of olive oil
1 hard-boiled egg, or 1 egg microwaved for 1 minute
1/4 of a piece of dry toast

CHOP egg finely with a fork.

ADD garlic powder and powdered milk while blending

together with a fork.

CRUMBLE the dry toast into little pieces and gradually add to the mix along with the olive oil.

Voila! Makes 1 serving.

Note: If still too dry, add a little water or chicken broth.

"Thousands of years ago, cats were worshipped as Gods. Cats have never forgotten this."

Anonymous

Cheese Please Cat Biscuits

Prep Time: 4 minutes   Bake Time: 20 minutes

Will make a cat come back for more!

1 cup of shredded Parmesan or cheddar cheese
3/4 cup of flour
1/2 cup of sour cream
1/2 cup of cornmeal
1 egg

MIX ingredients well. Form dough into 12 - 15 ball shapes.

PLACE balls on greased cookie sheet, then flatten each ball into a cookie. Place in preheated 350° F oven.

BAKE for 20 minutes or until brown. Cool, then serve. Yummy!

"The really great thing about cats is their endless variety. One can pick a cat to fit almost any decor, color scheme, income, personality, or mood. But under that fur, whatever color it may be, there still lies, essentially unchanged, one of the world's free souls."

Eric Gurney

Crabmeat Crème Brulee

Prep Time: 4 minutes   BakeTime: 25 - 28 minutes

A fine dining dessert custom made for our cat-kids!

1 cup of milk or soy milk
3 eggs whipped
1/2 cup of cooked crabmeat (canned
Chicken of the Sea recommended)
Note: Dab cream cheese on top of custard after
cooled.

MIX ingredients well and pour into
oven-tempered custard bowls.
PLACE into preheated
375° F oven.
BAKE for 25 - 28 minutes. Cool and scoop onto the pet
bowl and serve. Best to refrigerate leftovers for another
treat day, or share with the neighbor's cat!

*"By associating with the cat,
one only risks becoming
richer."*

Colette

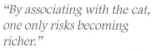

Crunchy Lobster Bisque Soup

Prep Time: 2 minutes   Cooking Time: 2 minutes

Not just for pet parents but shared with our pet-children too!

1 can of tomato soup
1 cup (or can) of milk or soy milk
2 tablespoons of your family's choice of crunchy cat food
1/2 cup of cooked (preferably boiled) lobster meat

MIX all ingredients together, except the crunchy cat food. Stir in a saucepan on the stove until warm, but not hot.

POUR into a bowl and sprinkle the crunchy cat food on top. Serve! Makes 2 large bowls.

"Cat's motto: No matter what you've done wrong, always try to make it look like the dog did it!"

Unknown

Easy~Make Cat and Kitty Cut~Out Treats

Prep Time: 5 minutes   Bake Time: 15 ~ 18 minutes

Simple to make and nutritious to eat!

1 cup of mashed sardine or flake canned tuna
1/2 cup of nonfat dry milk
1 egg
1/4 cup of wheat germ
4 tablespoons of flour

MIX all ingredients together.

ROLL dough out on a floured surface. Add additional flour as needed to make the dough stiff. Flatten dough out to about 1/2 inch thick and use cookie cut-outs for treats or make into cookies. Place shapes on a greased cookie sheet and put in a preheated 350° F oven.

BAKE for 15 ~ 18 minutes. Cool, then serve. Refrigerate leftovers.

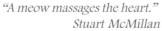

"A meow massages the heart."
Stuart McMillan

Fish Party Chips

Prep Time: 5 minutes   Bake Time: 20 - 23 minutes

Great snack treat ... one at a time!

1 cup of flaked tuna or canned salmon
2 tablespoons of melted butter
1-1/2 cups of whole wheat flour
3/4 cup of warm water

Cats

MASH canned tuna or salmon with a fork.
COMBINE with water, butter, and flour to form
dough. Separate dough into 20 pieces and form into flat
chip shapes. Place shapes on ungreased cookie sheet in a
preheated 325° F oven.
BAKE for 20 - 23 minutes or until lightly browned.
Cool, then serve. Refrigerate leftovers for another day!

Happy Holidays
Cat Cheese Balls

Prep Time: 4 minutes   Bake Time: 20 - 23 minutes

Great for special occasions for our pet-family members!

3/4 cup of grated cheddar cheese
3 tablespoons of softened, or melted, butter or margarine
3/4 cup of flour
1/2 teaspoon of catnip
or parsley
1 egg

MIX all ingredients together,
then roll into 12 small balls.

PLACE cheese balls onto a
greased cookie sheet and put in a preheated
350° F oven.

BAKE for 20 - 23 minutes. Cool, then serve. Voila!

Makes 1 dozen cheese balls.

*"Who can believe that there is
no soul behind those luminous
eyes!"*

Theophile Gautier

Icy Paw Claws

Prep Time: 1 minute

A cooling treat for a kitty after a hot day laying in the sun.

1/2 cup of plain or vanilla yogurt
1 6-ounce can of tuna in water, or canned shredded chicken
2 teaspoons of garlic powder

MIX all ingredients together, then place mixture in an ice tray.

FREEZE overnight, then serve. Note: you can add veggies or mashed bananas for that finicky eater in your house!

Cats

"Ever consider what they must think of us? I mean, here we come back from a grocery store with the most amazing haul - chicken, pork, half a cow. They must think we're the greatest hunters on earth!"
Anne Tyler

Jello Shrimp Treat

Prep Time: 3 minutes   Chill Time: 3 hours

Beat feet for a neat treat! Dogs and cats both love to eat!!

1 4-ounce package of Knox Gelatin, unflavored
1 cup of chicken stock
1/2 cup of cooked shrimp or canned shrimp pieces

FOLLOW gelatin box directions, exchanging the chicken stock for the cold water.

ADD shrimp or shrimp pieces.

POUR jello mixture into a square pan, OR use a variety of jello molds, such as hearts or egg shapes (can be bought where jello is sold).

CHILL for 3 hours, then cut into small pieces and serve. Refrigerate leftovers.

Cats

"To live long, eat like a cat, drink like a dog."
German proverb

Kitten Treat Delight

Prep Time: 2 minutes

High marks for this dinner sure to make the grade!

1 tablespoon of milk
1 egg beaten
1/3 cup of preferred dry kitten food, crushed
1/3 cup of softened cooked carrot slices (best microwaved for 1 minute)

MIX all ingredients together, then fold in the carrots.
BLEND well. Serve immediately. Refrigerate leftovers.
Great source of protein!

"I love cats because I love my home and after a while they become its visible soul."

Jean Cocteau

Kitty Cat
"Freedom" Toast Bites

Prep Time: 3 minutes   Cooking Time: 4 minutes
(2 minutes each side)

A sure way of getting your cat to join you for meal time, not just for breakfast time!

1 egg
1 slice of bread (whole wheat or white)
1/4 cup of milk
3 tablespoons of canned tuna

MIX egg, milk, and tuna in a bowl.

PLACE bread in bowl of egg mixture, flipping sides until bread is saturated.

COOK "Freedom" Toast in greased pan over the stove, flipping until sides are brown. Cool, then cut in small pieces and serve. Refrigerate leftovers.

"It's better to feed one cat than many mice."
Norwegian Proverb

Kitty Healthy Biscuits

Prep Time: 4 minutes   Bake Time: 20 - 25 minutes

For breakfast, lunch, or dinner!

1 cup of Bisquick mix
1/2 pound of cooked chicken livers or hearts, sliced into small pieces
1/2 cup of milk
1 egg
1/4 cup of cod liver oil

MIX all ingredients well. Form into balls and flatten each ball onto a greased cookie sheet. Place in preheated 350° F oven.

BAKE for 20 - 25 minutes or until golden brown. Cool, then serve. Makes 1 dozen biscuits.

"Dogs have owners. Cats have staff."
Unknown

Kitty Cat Healthy Shake

Prep Time: 4 minutes

A great shake to make for cats that need a little extra health boost in their diets!

1 cup of milk or soy milk
1/2 cup of tuna
1 tablespoon of kelp
1 egg (great for shiny coats)

BLEND all ingredients together in a blender. Serve!
Makes 1 serving.
Note: As an option add 1/4 cup of bovine colostrum powder (found at health food stores)

Purr-fect present!

Liver Lovin' Brownies

Prep Time: 5 minutes   Bake Time: 18 - 20 minutes

Cats and kittens will come back for more!

1/4 cup to 1/2 cup of cooked chicken livers, sliced
1 cup of wheat germ or cream of wheat cereal
1 cup of cornmeal
2 eggs
2 tablespoons of minced garlic
1/2 cup of milk

BLEND or puree in a blender for 1 minute.

POUR into a greased 9"x9" pan and place in a pre-heated 375° F oven.

BAKE for 18 - 20 minutes. Cool, then cut into portion sizes and serve. Refrigerate leftovers.

"Prowling his own quiet back-yard or asleep by the fire, he is still only a whisker away from the wilds."

Jean Burden

Meow Bon~Bons

Prep Time: 5 minutes   Bake Time: 18 ~ 20 minutes

Keep 'em happy! Keep 'em sweet. Treats cats love to eat and eat!

2 tablespoons of molasses
3 tablespoons of softened butter or margarine
2/3 cup of powdered nonfat milk
1~1/2 cups of whole wheat flour
2 teaspoons of catnip
2 eggs
3 teaspoons of wheat germ
2/3 cup of milk

MIX all ingredients well.

DROP by rounded teaspoon onto a greased cookie sheet. Place in preheated 350° F oven.

BAKE for 18 ~ 20 minutes. Cool, dab on cream cheese, then serve. Makes 2 dozen small bon~bons.

Munchy, Crunchy Mackerel Treats

Prep Time: 4 minutes   Bake Time: 8 - 10 minutes

Tasty, healthy and fun to make!

1 6-ounce can of canned mackerel, drained
2 eggs
1/2 cup of bread crumbs or crushed salad croutons
2 tablespoons of flour
2 tablespoons of vegetable or cod liver oil

MASH the mackerel with a fork, then combine the remaining ingredients.

DROP by spoonful onto greased cookie sheet. Place in preheated 375° F oven.

BAKE for 8 - 10 minutes. Cool, then serve. Store in refrigerator. Makes 1 dozen treats.

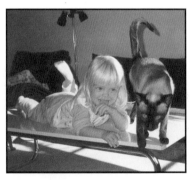

"When I play with my cat, who knows if I am not a pastime to her more than she to me?"

Montaigne

Shrimp Boat

Prep Time: 3 minutes

Sharing a snack with our pet-children puts a smile on our whole family's face

2 cut-up shrimp
1 cup of cottage cheese
1/4 cup of crushed dry cat food
1/2 celery stalk, finely chopped

MIX all ingredients well.
SERVE immediately.. and listen for the purring to begin. Makes 1 serving.

"After dark, all cats are leopards."
Native American proverb (Zuni)

Tuffy's Muffins

Prep Time: 4 minutes   Bake Time: 15 minutes

3 cubes of chicken bouillon
1/2 cup of warm water
2-1/2 cups of whole
wheat flour or rice flour
1 teaspoon of salt
1 cup of milk
2 eggs
1 tablespoon of vegetable
oil or cod liver oil

MIX all ingredients well. Pour into greased muffin pans filling 3/4 full. Place in preheated 375°F oven.
BAKE for 15 minutes, or until toothpick comes out clean. Cool, then serve. Makes 1 dozen small muffins.

"God made the cat that man might have the pleasure of caressing the tiger."
Ferdinand Mery

Tune Into Your Cat Cookies

Prep Time: 5 minutes   Bake Time: 10 - 12 minutes

Cats just love these cookies. Soft cookie treat--great for older cats!

1 can of flake tuna
1/2 cup of mashed green beans
2 tablespoons of vegetable oil or cod liver oil
2 eggs beaten
1 cup of nonfat dry milk
1/2 cup of water
2 cups of whole wheat flour
Note: To make it more tasty, dab on cream cheese when the cookies cool

MIX all ingredients well, and blend with a fork. Form dough into small balls, then flatten into cookies and place on an ungreased cookie sheet. Put in preheated 350° F oven.

BAKE for 10 - 12 minutes until golden brown. Cool, then serve. Refrigerate leftovers or share with a purr-fect neighbor's cat. Makes 2 dozen cookies.

"You will always be lucky if you know how to make friends with strange cats."
Colonial/American Proverb

Tuna Egg Bites

Prep Time: 3 minutes   Bake Time: 18 - 20 minutes

Cats go bonkers for this treat!

1 (6-ounce) can of flaked tuna
1 cooked egg (scrambled)
1/2 cup of cornmeal
1/2 cup of flour
1 egg

MIX all ingredients well, then form into balls.

PLACE tuna balls on a greased cookie sheet, and put in a preheated 350° F oven.

BAKE for 18 - 20 minutes. Makes 1 dozen cookies.

"The cat is the mirror of his human's mind, personality and attitude, just as the dog mirrors his human's physical appearance."
Winifred Carriere

Cats

Turkey Tidbits

Prep Time: 3 minutes   Bake Time: 20 - 25 minutes

Gobble, gobble... cats love 'em! Leftover turkey can be used in this recipe.

1/2 cup of beef or chicken stock
1 cup of cooked turkey, cut up in bite-sized pieces
1/2 cup of grated cheddar cheese
1/4 cup of melted butter or margarine
2 cups of flour
1 egg

MIX all ingredients well.

ROLL out dough and cut with cookie cutter, or drop by teaspoonful onto greased cookie sheet. Place in preheated 350° F oven.

BAKE for 20 - 25 minutes. Cool, then serve. Makes about 1 dozen tasty tidbits!

Vegi~Bits

Prep Time: 5 minutes   Bake Time: 30 minutes

3 cups of flour
1 cup of powdered milk
3/4 cup of vegetable oil
3 tablespoons of brown sugar
1/2 cup of cream of mushroom soup
1/2 cup of water
2 eggs

MIX all ingredients well, then form into balls.

PLACE on an ungreased cookie sheet. Put in preheated

300° F oven.

BAKE for 30 minutes. Makes 2 dozen Vegi-Bits.

"No matter how much cats fight, there always seems to be plenty of kittens."

Abraham Lincoln

Victory Veggie Vittles

Prep Time: 5 minutes   Bake Time: 10 ~ 12 minutes

Healthy and tasty, too! Great for vegetarian families.

1/2 cup of applesauce
1 cup of grated carrots or sliced green beans
1 egg, beaten
1 cup of cooked rice
1/2 cup of clear broth or water
1/4 cup of flour

MIX all ingredients well.
DROP by rounded teaspoon onto a greased cookie sheet, and place cookie sheet in preheated 350° F oven.
BAKE for 10 ~ 12 minutes. Cool, then serve. Best refrigerated after seving. Makes about 1~1/2 dozen vittles.

*There's a MEOW in the middle
of Homeowner!*

THE SMILING PETS™

"The greatness of a nation can be
judged by the way its animals
are treated."
                                        Mahatma Gandhi

"A good man or woman will take care of their horses and dogs not only while they are young, but also when they are old and past service."

Author Unknown

Peppermint Breath
Horse Muffins

Meaty Crunchy
Dog Bones

"Whoever said a horse was dumb,
was dumb."

Will Rogers

Pet Families

Mint Coconut
Doggie Breath Biscuits

Healthy Pet Shake

"For those who love it,
cooking is at once child's
play and adult joy. And
cooking done with care is
an act of love."

Craig Claiborn

Our salute to Chief Ron Lyons along with the Crystal Lake Park District Police Department "working dogs" Kasey and Chief. As representative of all the working dogs whose job is protection, search and rescue, education... we honor you!

Celebration Cake

"The Working Dog"

My eyes are your eyes,
To watch and protect
yours.

My ears are your ears,
To hear and detect evil
minds in the dark.

My nose is your nose,
To scent the invader of
your domain.

And so you may live,
My life is also yours.

Author Unknown

81

Just a ♪ to say:

Dear Smiling Pets,

I have always believed that I don't want them (my cats) eating my food and I don't want to eat theirs UNLESS it's a treat recipe from

THE SMILING PETS
Recipe Book

Let the feast begin!
Yumm! Yumm!
Yumeowee!
Love,
CC

UNCONDITIONAL LOVE, UNCONDITIONALLY

Music by Carol Connors
Lyrics by Carol Connors &
Mark Siegal

Chorus
Unconditional Love
Someone who appreciates me
Unconditional Love
Just my shadow and me

Carol Connors &
*NLYRICS, as photo-
graphed for the December
2002 cover of The Pet
Tribune, The Magazine
for Florida Pet Lovers.
Photographed by Timothy
Fielding. All Rights
Reserved.

We go everywhere
His Love's always there for me
Unconditional love,
Unconditionally...

When the world is comin' down on me
He's there for me, cares for me
When my life feels like I'm down and out
He turns my heart inside out

Unconditional Love
Never ever have to call his name
Unconditional Love
My friends always the same...

Chorus
Unconditional Love
Someone who appreciates me
Unconditional Love
Just my shadow and me

Smiling Pet Families

"No animal I know of can consistently be more of a friend and companion than a dog."

Stanley Leinwoll

"I love you not only for what you are, but for what I am when I am with you."

Roy Croft

Treats Please!

Horse Treats

Your horse loves you, not for your looks, but for your love! And food!

He knows when you're happy
He knows when you're comfortable
He knows when you're confident
And he ALWAYS knows when you have carrots or treats
Unknown

Apple Snax

Prep Time: 1 minute

Horse reward treat, healthy to eat!

1 large cored apple
1 chopped carrot
1/2 cup of oats

FILL cored apple with carrot and oats. Ready to serve!

*Rewards come with
accomplishments!*

American Pie Apple Mash

Prep Time: 4 minutes

Just the smell of apple mash will lead them your way...

3 large chopped apples
1 cup of molasses
1 cup of oatmeal
1 package of dry apple cider mix
1/2 cup of warm water
1/2 cup of bran cereal
1 cup of sweet feed

MIX all ingredients, except powdered cider mix.
POUR apple cider mix over ingredients in a bucket.
Serve! Um-mum.

Who among us has not asked for a pony on Christmas day?

Blue Ribbon Cake Treat

Prep Time: 5 minutes   Bake Time: 15 ~ 18 minutes

An award-winning treat for all the winners in your home!

5 peppermint sticks or pinwheels, finely crushed
1/2 cup of molasses
2 cups of oats
2 apples finely chopped
1 small banana mashed
1 carrot, minced
1 cup of water
1 cup of flour
2 eggs

MIX all ingredients together.

POUR into a 9"x9" greased pan and place in a preheated 350° F oven.

BAKE for 15 ~ 18 minutes, or until brown. Cool, then break apart and serve in a bucket with sprinkled sugar on top.

...always remember it is the treat that teaches the horse, not the consequences.

Candied Apple Balls

Prep Time: 2 minutes

Not just for the holidays... it's an anytime gift for your horse.

1 large apple
1/2 cup of molasses
1/2 cup of Rice Krispies cereal
1/2 cup of miniature marshmallows

POUR molasses over apple.

ROLL apple with molasses into Rice Krispies cereal and marshmallows, then serve!

"A horse gallops with its lungs, perseveres with its heart, and wins with its character."

Tessio

Caramel Apple Kiss

Prep Time: 2 minutes

Not just for the fair, caramel apples are a treat for a job well done!

1 medium apple
6 individual pieces of caramel
1/2 cup of Cheerios cereal
1/2 cup of chopped nuts

OPTIONAL Top off with carrot pieces

HEAT caramel pieces over a stove or microwave until melted.

POUR over apple and sprinkle on cereal/nut mixture. Chill and serve! Voila!

My Little Stud Muffins

Prep Time: 4 minutes   Bake Time: 28 - 30 minutes

Almost makes him smile when he sees me coming to greet him with this treat!

3/4 cup of applesauce
3/4 cup of corn syrup
3/4 cup of molasses or honey
3 carrots, finely chopped or grated
1/4 cup of salt
2 cups of oats
1 quart of Nutrena Life Design Youth feed

MICROWAVE molasses and syrups together until runny.

COMBINE carrots, oats, salt, and applesauce in a bowl and mix well. Add the syrups.

ROLL into balls and place on greased cookie sheet, or fill muffin pan 3/4 full. Put in a preheated 350° F oven.

BAKE for 28 - 30 minutes. Cool, then serve! Yummy... Makes 2 dozen large cookies or 1 dozen muffins.

"The outside of a horse is good for the inside of a man."

Winston Churchill

Healthy as a Horse
Health Drink!

Prep Time: 4 minutes

Can be poured over a horse's normal food ration, or can be an energy boost for the day!

1-1/2 cups of milk (2% or soy milk)
1 chopped carrot
1 tablespoon of sugar
1 egg
1/2 chopped apple
Note: 4 tablespoons of Bovine Colostrum powder is recommended for extra protein. Can be found at any health food store.

MIX all ingredients and place in a blender.
BLEND on high for 1 minute, then serve!

Horses

"He has galloped through a young girl's dreams, added richness to grown women's lives and served men in war and strife."

Toni Robinson

Horse Licks Popsicle Treats

Prep Time: 4 minutes

*Horse tail waggin' good after a day of trail rides
or an equine event... anytime, any place!*

2 carrots, chopped into small pieces
1 apple, chopped into small pieces
1 cup of carrot juice
1/2 cup of apple juice
2 teaspoons of sugar

MIX all ingredients in a bowl.

POUR mixture into ice trays and freeze overnight.

SERVE in a bucket right away the next day!

*"Horses change lives. They give our young people
confidence and self-esteem..."*

Toni Robinson

Horses

Horsey Carrot Cookies

Prep Time: 3 minutes   Bake Time: 17 minutes

Great reward for a job well done... or just simply for their devotion to us!

1/2 cup of molasses
1 cup of flour
1 cup of carrots, shredded
1/2 cup of oats
1 teaspoon of honey
3 teaspoons of vegetable oil

MIX all ingredients together.

ROLL mixture into small dough balls and place on a greased cookie sheet. Put in preheated 350° F oven.

BAKE for 17 minutes, or until brown. Serve 2 to 3 at a time and store leftovers in the refrigerator. Makes about 1 dozen cookies.

Horse people are stable people.

Instant Spiced Oatmeal Cereal Snack

Prep Time: 3 minutes

Variety of treats is the spice of life!

2 packages of brown sugar or cinnamon spice instant oatmeal cereal mix
1/2 apple, finely chopped
1/2 cup of molasses or honey

FOLLOW instructions on instant oatmeal cereal package.

FOLD in apples and molasses or honey.

POUR into bucket. Cool, then serve.

"I took to the life of a cowboy like a horse takes to oats."

Clinton McCoy

Horses

Magic's Celery Stick Wand!

Prep Time: 1 minute

Healthy and fun to make "magic" treat... see how fast it disappears!

1 celery stalk
Peanut butter
Oats

COVER the celery stalk with peanut butter.
ROLL individual celery sticks in oats, then serve. Makes 1 serving.

"...the horse has been, of all animals, man's most constant companion in work and leisure."
from "Horses"

Marshmallow Apple Balls

Prep Time: 2 minutes

The whole "neigh"borhood will want this treat!
MULES, too!

1 cup of small marshmallows
1/3 cup of molasses
1/2 of an apple, chopped

OPTIONAL grapes

MIX all ingredients together. With butter or margarine coated hands, mold mixture into balls. Chill, then serve!

"If three people say you are an ass, put on a bridle."
Spanish proverb

PBJ Oat Cookies

Prep Time: 5 minutes   Bake Time: 15 - 18 minutes

Good in summer time, good anytime!

1 cup of oats
1/2 cup of peanut butter
2 cups of flour
1/2 cup of strawberry jam or jelly
1/2 cup of water
1 egg
1 teaspoon of baking soda

MIX all ingredients well.

POUR more water, if needed, to make a consistency like cookie dough.

ROLL dough into large tablespoon-sized balls. Place on greased cookie sheet and put in preheated 375° F oven.

BAKE for 15 - 18 minutes. Cool, then serve. Makes 1 to 1-1/2 dozen large cookies.

Horses

"Care, and not fine stables, make a good horse."
        Danish proverb

Peanut Butter Pie Treat

Prep Time: 3 minutes

*Super reward for a well done ride, trail, racing, or
leisure stroll...*

1 cup of oatmeal
2 large chopped apples
1 grated large carrot
1 cup of peanut butter
1/2 cup of sugar

MICROWAVE (or melt in a small sauce pan)
peanut butter until runny or creamy.
MIX carrots, apples, and oats in a pie pan.
POUR peanut butter over the above ingredients.
Sprinkle sugar on top, then serve!

*"Courage is being scared to death and
saddling up anyway."*

John Wayne

Peppermint Breath Horse Muffins

Prep Time: 5 minutes   Bake Time: 25 ~ 28 minutes

Fresh breath and yummy, too... 2 treats in one!

4-6 crushed red and white pinwheel peppermints
1 apple, finely chopped
2 tablespoons of honey
2 cups of oats
2 cups of flour
3 tablespoons of brown sugar
2 eggs
1 teaspoon of baking soda

MIX all ingredients well.

POUR into greased muffin tin. Place in a preheated 350° F oven.

BAKE for 25 ~ 28 minutes. Cool, then serve. Your horse will love you for this! Makes about 1 dozen muffins.

Horses

Horses give us wings we lack.

Trigger's Rice Cakes

Prep Time: 3 minutes

Easy to make and store for a quick and healthy treat after a horse trail ride, or anytime!

1 plain rice cake
1/2 carrot cut in pieces
1/2 apple cut in pieces
1/4 cup of molasses

POUR molasses over rice cake.
DECORATE like a pizza using the remaining ingredients. Serve! Makes 1 serving.

"We found that the best use for his candy was lurin' your horse in the morning."

Bill Craig

Strawberry Salad Pie

Prep Time: 3 minutes

Summertime refreshing treat!

1 cup of chopped strawberries
1 cup of oats
1 chopped carrot
1 cup of chopped celery
1 cup of molasses

MIX fruit and veggies together.

POUR molasses over the fruit and veggies, and stir.

Ready to serve!

"Spending that many hours in the saddle gave a man plenty of time to think. That's why so many cowboys fancied themselves philosophers."

C.M. Russel

Trixi's Trail Mix

Prep Time: 3 minutes

Can be stored in baggies for a little bit of a treat, a bit at a time. Mules love this, too!

1 cup of Cheerios or Raisin Bran cereal
3 apples, chopped in small pieces
2 stalks of celery, cut up
3 carrots chopped in small pieces
1 cup of oatmeal

MIX together all ingredients in a bucket, and serve.

"There's nothing better for the soul of a man, or young man, than the outside of a horse..."
Ronald Reagan

Tuity Fruity Sweet Treat

Prep Time: 3 minutes

A nice change of pace... yum yum, watermelon!

1 cup of watermelon (cut off the rind)
1 chopped apple
1 large carrot, cut up
1 tablespoon of sugar or sugar cubes

MIX fruit and carrot in a bucket. Add sugar and stir until it dissolves.

SERVE and enjoy the accolades!

"Don't change horses while crossing a stream."
American Proverb

Wintertime Mish Mash

Prep Time: 3 minutes

A delicious source of protein to maintain weight during a cold winter's night.

1 cup of beet pulp (best if pellets soaked overnight)
1/2 cup of vegetable oil
1 cup of Sweet Feed
1/2 cup of oats

MIX all ingredients well in a bucket. Serve!

"A pony is a childhood dream, a horse is an adulthood treasure."

Rebecca Carroll

Bird Treats

Lessons from Geese

As each goose flaps its wings it creates an "uplift" for the bird that follows. By flying in a V formation, the whole flock adds 71% greater range than if each bird flew alone.

When a goose falls out of formation, it suddenly feels the draft of flying alone. It quickly moves back into formation to take advantage of the lifting power of the bird in front of it.

When the lead goose tires, it rotates back into the formation as another goose flies to the point position.

The geese flying in formation honk to encourage those up front to keep up their speed.

When a goose gets sick, wounded or shot down, two geese drop out of formation and follow it down to help protect it. They stay with it until it dies or is able to fly again. Then they launch out with another formation or catch up with the flock.

                                                            -Author Unknown

Blueberry~Cherry Jubilee Suet

Prep Time: 5 minutes

The wild birds can now enjoy berries all through the winter months... our treat!

3 cups of melted rendered suet
1/2 cup of frozen blueberries (or fresh when in season)
1/2 cup of pitted cherries
1/2 cup of sunflower seeds and/or cracked corn
1 slice of toasted whole wheat bread, crumbled
OR 1 cup of salad croutons

MIX all ingredients in a mixing bowl. Stir until the bread is soaked.

POUR into a round pie pan or form into a block. Chill for 30 minutes, then hang for the birds to enjoy!

"Use what talent you possess: the woods would be very silent if no birds sang except those that sang best."
Henry Van Dyke

Birds

Bye-Bye Birdie Oatmeal Muffin Suet Cakes

Prep Time: 4 minutes

Watch the birdies flock over these cakes!

3 cups of melted rendered suet
1/2 cup of sunflower seeds
1/2 cup of peanut butter
1/2 cup of cornmeal
1/2 cup of oats

MIX all ingredients in a mixing bowl, and blend well.
POUR into paper-lined muffin tin. Chill and serve to
the birdies. Makes about 4 to 5 muffin suets.

*"Be like the bird that passing on her flight while on boughs too slight,
feels them give way beneath her, and yet sings, knowing that she has
wings!"*

Victor Hugo

Cherry Pie Suet Treats

Prep Time: 4 minutes

Great craft idea for scouts, bible schools and seniors.
It is always well received!

6 pitted cherries
1 cup of sunflower seeds or cracked corn
1/2 cup thistle seeds
3 cups melted suet

MIX all ingredients in a mixing bowl.

POUR into a square tin to form for suet holder.

CHILL until firm, then place in holder for the birds to devour.

"I value my garden more for being full of
blackbirds than of cherries... and very frankly
give them fruit for their songs."

Joseph Addison

Cookie Dough Suet

Prep Time: 4 minutes

Even birdies like a change in treats once in a while!

2 cups of melted rendered suet
1/2 cup of chopped up carob (looks like chocolate chips but is a healthy root; found in health food stores)
1/2 cup of wheat flour
1 cup of cornmeal

MIX all ingredients together.
POUR the dough into a pie pan (disposable tin is great)
CHILL until firm, and serve to the birdies.

"The mother eagle teaches her little ones to fly by making their nest so uncomfortable that they are forced to leave it and commit themselves to the unknown world of air outside. And just so does our God to us. He stirs up our comfortable nests, and pushes us over the edge of them, and we are forced to use our wings to save ourselves from fatal falling. Read your trials in this light, and see if you cannot begin to get a glimpse of their meaning. Your wings are being developed."

Hannah Whithall Smith

Birds

Granola Health Bar Suet

Prep Time: 3 minutes

A delicious healthy treat for the birds on your street!

2 cups of melted suet
1 crushed granola bar
1/2 cup of crunchy peanut butter
1/2 cup of cornmeal

MICROWAVE (or melt in a sauce pan on the stove) suet and peanut butter until runny.

MIX with granola and cornmeal, and pour into a freezer storage container or an empty clean soup can to freeze. Once firm, scoop out or place outside for birds to nibble on the "tweets."

*"Hope is the thing with feathers
That perches in the soul,
And sings the tune without the words,
And never stops at all."*
                    Emily Dickinson

Birds

Peanut Birdie Suet Cakes

Prep Time: 3 minutes

Tweet to eat!

2 cups of melted rendered suet
1/2 cup of peanut butter
1/2 cup of cornmeal
sprinkle seasonal bird seed on top

MELT suet and peanut butter, then add cornmeal.
Sprinkle bird seed on top.
SPOON into disposable pie tin and cool. Ready to
serve and ready to eat.

*"One reason why birds and horses
are happy is because they are not
trying to impress other birds and
horses."*

Dale Carnegie,
How to Win Friends
and Influence People

Birds

Pinecone Quick Feeder

Prep Time: 4 minutes

Great gift to give the birdwatchers in your family...
tweet, tweet, tweet!

2 cups of rendered suet or bacon/beef grease drippings
1 slice of whole wheat bread
1/4 cup of cornmeal
1/2 cup of shelled sunflower seeds

MELT suet and dip or dab onto (and into) crevices of the pinecone. Make sure pinecone has an attached hanger for the tree.

PRESS bread into crevices of the pinecone.

SPRINKLE cornmeal and seeds generously over pinecone.

HANG on the tree and watch the birds surround it and devour the treats.

"If you want to soar with the eagles in the morning, you can't hoot with the owls all night."

Anonymous

Woody Woodpecker Log Suet

Prep Time: 3 minutes

Helping nature feed the birds is the only natural way to go...

1 (1-foot) log, untreated wood. Drill holes 1-inch in diameter for
suet mix to sit in
2 cups of melted rendered suet
1/2 cup of bacon or beef bits finely chopped, or beef jerky pieces
1/4 cup of cornmeal

MIX all ingredients together.

PUSH suet mix into the 1 inch diameter holes in the log.

HANG log in a tree on a branch for the woodpecker to enjoy.

"Even the woodpecker owes his success to the fact that he uses his head and keeps pecking away until he finishes the job he starts."

Coleman Cox

"There are two lasting bequests we can give our children: one is roots and the other is wings."

Hodding Carter, Jr.

Baby Food Confetti Cakes

Prep Time: 4 minutes   Bake Time: 15 - 18 minutes

Sweet Potato Pie, oh my, oh my!

1 (6-ounce) jar of baby food sweet potatoes
2 (4-ounce) jars of baby food fruit (kiwi or exotic fruits
recommended, but adjust to your pet's desires)
1-1/2 cups of bird Daily Feed pellets
3 eggs and cleaned egg shells crushed
3 packets of Cream of Wheat instant cereal

MIX all ingredients well, especially egg shells. Food
processor works well to achieve desired fine
dough consistency.

PLACE mixture in lightly greased muffin tin. Place in
preheated 375° F oven.

BAKE for 15 - 18 minutes or until golden brown. Let
cool, then serve.

*"A friend (and pet-mom) is someone
who knows the song in your heart and
can sing it back to you when you have
forgotten the words..."*

Unknown

Birds

Fruity Bird Cookies

Prep Time: 5 minutes   Bake Time: 20 - 25 minutes

All our pet-children, including birds, love cookies...
and you can make them healthy, too!

1/2 cup of dried fruit (such as apricots, bananas, apples,
figs, or a variety of all)
2 eggs
1/2 cup of peanut butter,
smooth or chunky
1/2 cup of wheat flour
1/3 cup of bird crushed pellets
2 crushed peppermints

MIX all ingredients well. If
you choose to add egg shells, make sure they are
finely ground.

DROP by tablespoon on lightly greased cookie sheet,
and place in a preheated 375° F oven.

BAKE for 20 - 25 minutes. Cool, then serve. Best to
refrigerate leftovers for another treat day! Makes 1
dozen cookies.

*"Live in such a way that you
would not be ashamed to
give your parrot to the town
gossip."*

Will Rogers

PBJ Pinecone Exotic
Bird Treat

Prep Time: 3 minutes

Exotic Pet birds love a variety of treats!

4 tablespoons of chunky peanut butter
2 tablespoons of strawberry jam
1 large pine cone
2 tablespoons of raisins
1/2 cup of daily bird seed

Note: This treat can be customized to the
individual taste of your pet bird. Add or omit
to your pet's hearts desire. Do not feed
chocolate or avacado to birds because it
can be toxic to them.

ATTACH a twist-tie around the pinecone so that it
will adhere to a pet bird cage.

SMEAR peanut butter and jelly liberally over
the pinecone.

DIP peanut butter pinecone in seeds, raisins and any
other favorite bird snack food.

Popcorn Birdie Treasure Chest

Prep Time: 5 minutes

A great way to hide birdie vitamins and still treat your pet!

4 cups of air-popped popcorn
2 tablespoons of margarine or butter
1 (6-ounce) package of Sun Maid fruit bits or 1/2 cup of finely
chopped dried fruit
Bird vitamins
1 teaspoon of cinnamon

POP air popcorn.

MELT butter or margarine. Add cinnamon fruit and vitamins.

TOSS the popcorn and fruit mixture together in a paper bag. Shake bag until well saturated, then serve!

"It is not only fine feathers that make fine birds."

Aesop

Birds

Sweet Tweet Bird Balls

Prep Time: 4 minutes

A smorgasbord treat sure to please the singer, the talker, but more importantly, the pet-bird in your pet-family!

6 graham crackers, finely crushed
1-1/2 cups of peanut butter, chunky or smooth
4 tablespoons of honey
1/2 cup of finely chopped walnuts
1 cup of wheat germ or Cream of Wheat cereal dry mix
1 cup of raisins and/or dry fruit of your
pet-child's choice
1/2 cup of shredded coconut

MIX all ingredients together, except coconut.

FORM into balls and roll in coconut.

CHILL for 1/2 hour until firm, then serve. Refrigerate leftovers to serve another day! Makes 6 large or 12 small treat balls.

"A bird does not sing because it has an answer. It sings because it has a song."

Chinese proverb

Birds

121

★*A Pet-Mom's Creed*★

"To laugh often and much; to win the respect of intelligent people and the affection of children (and pet-children); to earn the appreciation of honest critics and endure the betrayal of false friends; to appreciate beauty, to find the best in others; to leave the world a little better; whether by a healthy child, a garden patch or a redeemed social condition; to know even one life has breathed easier because you have lived. This is the meaning of success."

Ralph Waldo Emerson

Index

Making Tracks...

Animal Planet TV
Beverly Hills Vet Segment

Totally Pets
with Cyndy Garvey
ABC Family Channel

Cooking with
Jackie Olden
In conjuction with the Palm
Springs, CA animal shelter
adoption program.
UPN 13

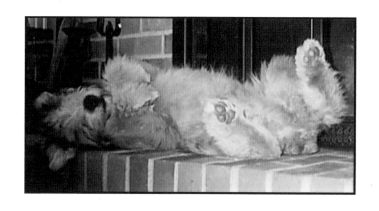

The End